TRADITIONS AND CELEBRATIONS

YOM KIPPUR

by Emily Raij

PEBBLE
a capstone imprint

Published by Pebble, an imprint of Capstone
1710 Roe Crest Drive, North Mankato, Minnesota 56003
capstonepub.com

Library of Congress Cataloging-in-Publication Data is available on the Library of Congress website.

ISBN: 9798875219894 (hardcover)
ISBN: 9798875219849 (paperback)
ISBN: 9798875219856 (ebook PDF)

Summary: Readers discover how Jewish people conclude the High Holy Days by considering the past, asking for forgiveness, and resolving to do better on Yom Kippur.

Editorial Credits
Editor: Kellie M. Hultgren; Designer: Elyse White; Media Researcher: Rebekah Hubstenberger; Production Specialist: Tori Abraham

Image Credits
Getty Images: Hans-Peter Merten, 1, iStock/cmspic, 10, iStock/demerzel, 21, 16, iStock/EyeJoy, 18, iStock/shironosov, 15, 21, iStock/tovfla, 11, iStock/tzahiV, 8, iStock/ultracoldsound, 22, Jerry Holt/Star Tribune, 9, MoMo Productions, 28, Pascal Deloche, 17, Rafael Ben-Ari, 19; Shutterstock: Anna_Pustynnikova, 25, antoniodiaz, 26, Brent Hofacker, 23, Galiyah Assan, 20, Gorodenkoff, 29, Joanna Dorota, 27, Kobby Dagan, 13, Noam Armonn, 14, PeopleImages.com - Yuri A, 7, Picture Partners, 24, Pixel-Shot, 6, Robophoto1, 5, vetre, cover

Design Elements
Shutterstock: Rafal Kulik

TABLE OF CONTENTS

Words in **bold** are in the glossary.

What Is Yom Kippur?

The hot days of summer have ended. Fall brings cooler weather. Kids go back to school. **Jewish** children get ready to celebrate fall holidays.

Yom Kippur is one of them. It takes place after Rosh Hashanah, the Jewish New Year. Together, Rosh Hashanah and Yom Kippur are the High **Holy** Days. Those are the holiest days of the year for Jewish people.

On Rosh Hashanah, apples and honey represent a sweet new year.

Jewish people believe God opens the Book of Life on Rosh Hashanah. This book shows how people acted all year. On Yom Kippur, Jews **reflect** on how they can improve. People ask God for **forgiveness**. They ask others to forgive them.

God listens to people's prayers. On the evening of Yom Kippur, the book is closed. This seals a person's **fate** for the year. Yom Kippur is also called the Day of Atonement. That means working to correct mistakes. It is a serious day when Jews think about doing better.

When Is Yom Kippur?

All Jewish holidays start at sundown. Yom Kippur ends the next night when three stars can be seen in the sky.

A Yom Kippur service in Minneapolis, Minnesota

Jewish holidays are based on a lunar calendar. It follows the phases of the moon. That means the holiday dates change each year. Sometimes Yom Kippur is in September. Other years it is in October. But Yom Kippur is always ten days after Rosh Hashanah.

Getting Ready

Jews prepare for Yom Kippur in many ways. They think about what they have done wrong. They say sorry to people they have hurt with their words or actions. They think of how to do better the next year. Many people also donate money to charity. Those gifts are called tzedakah.

A girl donates money in a tzedakah box.

Many Jewish adults do not work on Yom Kippur. They light candles. They say blessings over bread, and they thank God. Some people wear white during the holiday. It **symbolizes** a fresh start.

Jews wish each other "G'mar chatima tovah." That means "a good final sealing" of a person's fate in **Hebrew**. Hebrew is the language of the Jewish people.

Jewish men in white clothing and prayer shawls pray in the city of Jerusalem on Yom Kippur.

Yom Kippur is a serious day. People stop doing things that are fun or comforting. Many people fast. This means not eating or drinking. To get ready, they have a good dinner and drink plenty of water. Children and those who are sick, very old, or pregnant should not fast.

While they fast, Jews think about their actions. Being hungry does not feel good. It helps people think about how they hurt others. Then they can apologize.

A Day to Pray

Many Jews pray at a **synagogue** during Yom Kippur. Prayers start after dinner. A **rabbi** leads prayer services. Then everyone goes home.

Temple Emanu-El is a synagogue in New York City.

Reading the Torah during a prayer service

Services start again the next morning. They last all day. Some people take breaks to study the **Torah**, the Jewish holy book. Others take a nap.

There are different services. A memory service honors loved ones who died. Many people light a memory candle at home and pray.

A man plays the shofar.

A closing service ends with a long blast from the **shofar**. That is a ram's horn. It is played like a trumpet. The loud noise wakes people's spirits. It calls them to think about God and do better.

Holiday Foods Before and After

Challah is a braided bread Jews eat all year. It is made into a round shape for Rosh Hashanah and Yom Kippur. The shape symbolizes the cycle of the year. It also represents doing good with no end. Jews dip challah in honey for a sweet new year.

Challah

Before Yom Kippur, people get ready to fast. It is important to eat a good meal and drink lots of water before fasting.

Fasting ends at sundown. Then people eat a meal called a break-fast. It is often held at the synagogue or with family at home. The food was prepared before Yom Kippur. This joyful meal ends a serious holiday.

Kugel

Jews from different countries eat different foods. Ashkenazi Jews have **ancestors** from Eastern Europe. Ashkenazi Jews in North America often eat bagels, cream cheese, fish, fruits, vegetables, and kugel. Kugel is a sweet noodle casserole. People also eat sweets for a sweet year. Honey cake is a favorite.

Sephardic Jews have ancestors from Spain, Portugal, North Africa, and the Middle East. Some break the fast with omelets or slow-cooked eggs. Many eat soups, fish, and meat stews.

Harira soup is eaten after Yom Kippur in Morocco.

Mint tea

Jews from Morocco break the fast with mint tea and fried dough dipped in syrup. Persian Jews enjoy a drink made from apples and rosewater. It is very refreshing after a long fast!

Yom Kippur Actions

On Yom Kippur, people make goals to do better. They say sorry to people they have hurt.

Apologizing for hurting others is important on Yom Kippur.

   A good apology means saying sorry and asking for forgiveness. Fix what went wrong. Then promise not to do it again.

Some children make a list of goals for the year. They might want to be a better friend. They might plan to help out more at home. Children can also help others. They can donate toys and books to kids in need. They can donate to food pantries too.

People work on Yom Kippur goals all year. It is a time to improve yourself and help others. That makes the world better!

GLOSSARY

ancestor (AN-sess-tur)—a family member who lived a long time ago

fate (FAYT)—events in a person's life that are out of that person's control

forgiveness (for-GIV-niss)—the act of accepting someone's apology

Hebrew (HEE-broo)—a language used by ancient Israelites and modern-day Jewish people

holy (HO-lee)—dedicated to God or a religious purpose

Jewish (JOO-ish)—describing Judaism, a religion based on a belief in one God and the teachings of a holy book called the Torah

rabbi (RAB-EYE)—a teacher of Jewish law who is usually a leader of a congregation

reflect (ri-FLEKT)—to think deeply about something

shofar (SHOH-far)—a ram's horn that is blown like a trumpet in the Jewish religion

symbolizes (SIM-buh-liz-es)—stands for or represents something else

synagogue (SIHN-uh-gog)—a building where Jewish people come to pray

Torah (TOE-rah)—the law of God that makes up the first five books of the Hebrew Bible

READ MORE

Koster, Gloria. *Rosh Hashanah*. North Mankato, MN: Capstone, 2023.

Tierney, Peggy. *How to Change the World in 12 Easy Steps: Inspired by the Life Lessons of Eva Mozes Kor*. Indianapolis, IN: Tanglewood, 2021.

Vallepur, Shalini. *At the Synagogue*. King's Lynn, UK: BookLife, 2020.

INTERNET SITES

BBC Bitesize: What Is Yom Kippur?
bbc.co.uk/bitesize/articles/z4vvjhv

Britannica Kids: Yom Kippur
kids.britannica.com/kids/article/Yom-Kippur/353948

PJ Library: What Is Yom Kippur?
pjlibrary.org/beyond-books/pjblog/july-2020/what-is-yom-kippur

INDEX

ABOUT THE AUTHOR

Emily Raij has written more than forty books for children and edited dozens of professional resources for K–12 teachers. She is a native of Chicago, where she earned her journalism degree from Northwestern University. She lives in Florida with her husband, daughter, son, and dog.